# Science Matters! | Volume 8

# Habitats

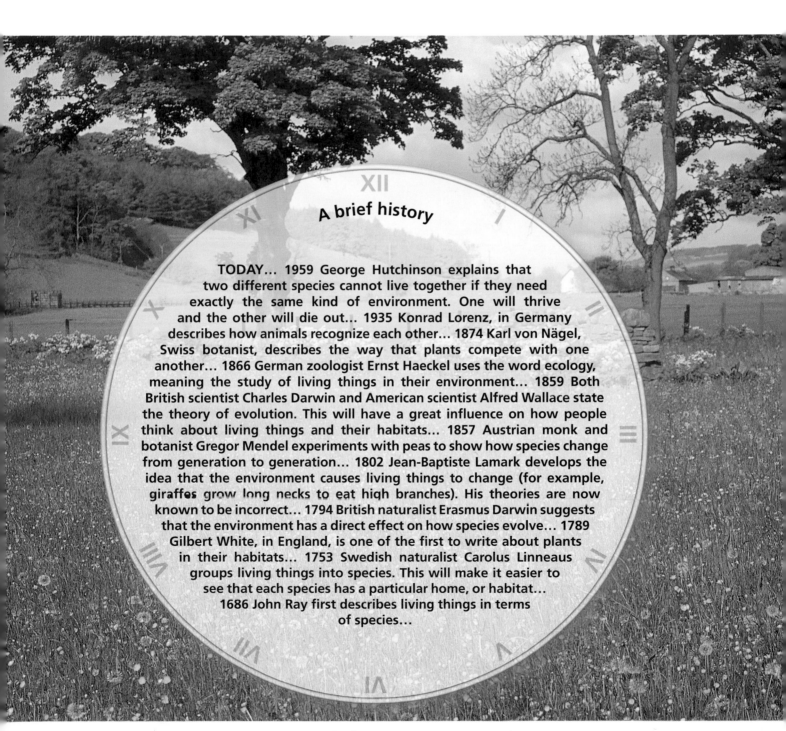

A brief history

TODAY... 1959 George Hutchinson explains that two different species cannot live together if they need exactly the same kind of environment. One will thrive and the other will die out... 1935 Konrad Lorenz, in Germany describes how animals recognize each other... 1874 Karl von Nägel, Swiss botanist, describes the way that plants compete with one another... 1866 German zoologist Ernst Haeckel uses the word ecology, meaning the study of living things in their environment... 1859 Both British scientist Charles Darwin and American scientist Alfred Wallace state the theory of evolution. This will have a great influence on how people think about living things and their habitats... 1857 Austrian monk and botanist Gregor Mendel experiments with peas to show how species change from generation to generation... 1802 Jean-Baptiste Lamark develops the idea that the environment causes living things to change (for example, giraffes grow long necks to eat high branches). His theories are now known to be incorrect... 1794 British naturalist Erasmus Darwin suggests that the environment has a direct effect on how species evolve... 1789 Gilbert White, in England, is one of the first to write about plants in their habitats... 1753 Swedish naturalist Carolus Linneaus groups living things into species. This will make it easier to see that each species has a particular home, or habitat... 1686 John Ray first describes living things in terms of species...

## Dr. Brian Knapp

# Word list

These are some science words that you should look out for as you go through the book. They are shown using CAPITAL letters.

**ADAPT/ADAPTATION**
The way in which an animal or plant is suited to where it lives. If something is well adapted to where it lives, it will be more likely to survive.

**CARNIVORE**
An animal that eats meat.

**CELL**
A basic building block of all living things. The simplest living things are made of a single cell. Very complicated living things, like people, are made of billions of cells. The more cells there are, the more the chances are that some cells will be specialized and form a more complicated living thing.

**COMMUNITY**
The range of living things that occur in the same habitat. For example, different communities of plants and animals will exist in a meadow, an oak wood, or a pond.

**ENERGY**
The "power pack" that makes it possible for living things to grow, move, etc.

**ENVIRONMENT**
The surroundings in which a living thing finds itself. It includes the type of soil, the shape of the land, the amount of warmth and rain, the amount of shelter, and the other plants and animals that share the same space.

**FOOD CHAIN**
A group of plants and animals that depend on each other for food. In general, plants need animals to help spread their pollen and seeds. Some animals need plants for food, while other animals need the plant-eaters for their food.

**HABITAT**
The place where an animal or plant normally lives. A habitat can be very small (for example, under a leaf),

or it may be very large (for example, a tropical rain forest).

**HERBIVORE**
An animal that eats plants for its food.

**MICROORGANISM**
An organism that can only be seen with a microscope, for example, a bacterium. They are also called microbes.

**ORGANISM**
The most general word for any living thing, including both plants and animals.

**PREDATOR**
An animal that hunts other animals for its food.

**PREY**
An animal that is hunted by other animals for food.

**SPECIES**
A group of living things that can breed with one another.

# Contents

# What are living things?

**Living things are those that can produce offspring. Any living thing is called an ORGANISM, but we usually call them by common names such as plants and animals.**

Everything in the world is either living or nonliving. An example of a living thing is a spider or a cactus or a human being. An example of a nonliving thing is a piece of rock or a computer. (We use the term nonliving instead of dead because for something to be dead, it must once have been alive. A nonliving thing has never been alive.)

Living things can be huge and easy to recognize as being alive, for example, a whale. At the other end of the scale living things can be so small that it takes a powerful microscope just to see them, as is the case with tiny creatures called bacteria.

It is not always easy to prove that some things are living. Look, for example, at a lichen (which is actually two different plantlike things growing very close together) growing on a stone (Picture 1). The lichen doesn't seem to move, is often dry and crisp to the touch, and grows by less than a millimeter a year,

▼ **(Picture 1) The difference between the lichen, which is the colored patch, and the rock is that the lichen is a living thing, while the rock is a nonliving thing.**

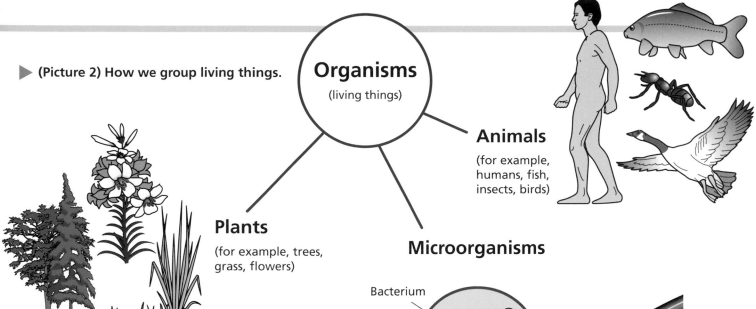

**Organisms**
(living things)

**Plants**
(for example, trees, grass, flowers)

**Animals**
(for example, humans, fish, insects, birds)

**Microorganisms**

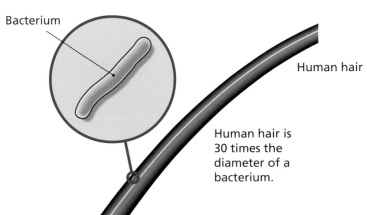

Bacterium

Human hair

Human hair is 30 times the diameter of a bacterium.

▲ (Picture 3) Microorganisms are tiny living things that have very simple bodies. This is a bacterium on a human hair.

so it looks much the same for a long time. In fact, to many people it would appear to be a nonliving thing, looking like a stain on the rock.

## What living things share

Lichens, humans, trees, whales, and all other living things have certain things in common:

▶ They take in food to make **ENERGY**.
▶ They give off waste products, even if only heat or a gas.
▶ They grow, even if slowly.
▶ They can move, even if only a little.
▶ They are affected by changes in the world around them (called their **ENVIRONMENT**).
▶ They change, or **ADAPT**, over time to suit their environment.
▶ They can make new living things (such as babies) of their own kind.

We can use this list to tell living things from nonliving things.

## Organisms

Scientists have a word for any living thing. It is organism. We tend to use more familiar words for many organisms, such as plant and animal or tree and whale (Picture 2). Very small organisms that can only be seen through a microscope are called **MICROORGANISMS**, which many people also call microbes (Picture 3).

**Summary**
• There are many different types of living things.
• All living things have some things in common.

# Eating, growing, moving, and changing

All living things need food for energy so they can carry on growing, moving, and changing.

All living things—all organisms—take in food or make their own food. Green plants, such as grass and trees, make their own food using sunlight, water, air, and substances in the soil. They then use this food to keep living, to grow, and to move.

Animals cannot make their own food, so they must eat food made by plants or other animals.

## How food is used

Food is used as a supply of energy, the power needed to allow living things to survive. For example, even if we lie perfectly still, we still need energy just to breathe, for our hearts to beat, and for blood to be pumped around our bodies.

We need more energy (and so more food) to build bigger bodies as we grow and to move around.

The bodies of all living things are really chemical factories where food is broken down, then rebuilt into things useful for life such as skin and bone, or used as energy.

## How living things grow and change

No matter how long you left a chair in a room, it would not change shape or move. But living things do both of these things (Pictures 1 and 2). How do they manage it? They do it by adding or changing the tiny building blocks all living things are made up of. We call these building blocks CELLS.

▶ (Picture 1) If you did not think that plants move, then you would be surprised by this sensitive plant. The fernlike leaves close as soon as they are touched.

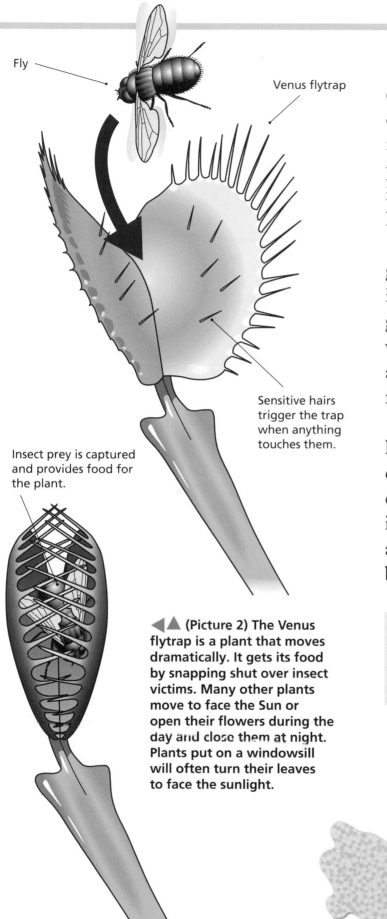

Fly

Venus flytrap

Sensitive hairs trigger the trap when anything touches them.

Insect prey is captured and provides food for the plant.

◀◀▲ (Picture 2) The Venus flytrap is a plant that moves dramatically. It gets its food by snapping shut over insect victims. Many other plants move to face the Sun or open their flowers during the day and close them at night. Plants put on a windowsill will often turn their leaves to face the sunlight.

The simplest living things are made of just one cell. When it is time for this cell to grow, it splits in two, and each new half grows up to be the size of its parent (Picture 3). All living things grow in this way, even humans whose bodies have billions of cells.

Having a body made of many cells gives the chance for some cells to grow in different ways. In plants some cells grow to be the building blocks of flowers, while others build stems and roots; in animals some cells build eyes, hands, feet, and so on.

Because even the most complicated living thing is made of many individual cells, it is possible for living things to change when the cells change. That is how we grow, and over time, how all living things change—or evolve—to best suit their environment.

## Summary
- All living things grow and change.
- All living things need food.
- All living things are made of cells.

◀ (Picture 3) Amebas are living things made of just one cell. They grow by splitting into two parts.

# Finding out where plants live

A habitat is the place where a living thing is best suited to live, and where it finds shelter, food, and others of its own kind.

Now we have seen that living things make use of their environment to get food, and that they can move and change, it is time to look at the environment around them.

A place where a living thing makes its home is called its **HABITAT**.

## Habitats

Habitats come in all shapes and sizes. There are microbes living in our bodies, in our eyes, ears, and so on. Most do you no harm, but to them an ear, a mouth, or an eye is home—it is their habitat.

On a larger scale a woodland is home to the trees that live there, but also to all of the other plants and the many animals that use it for food and shelter (Picture 1).

A rock pool by the sea, a pond, a river, or a coral reef are all watery habitats.

## Where dandelions live

To get used to finding out where something lives, you can begin by walking around close

Oak tree

Ivy climbing up tree in shade.

Ferns in shade.

**(Picture 1) As you move from a woodland to a meadow and then to a pond, you will find different things making their home in each place. Each place is a different habitat.**

Brambles partially shaded and partly in sunny areas.

SHADE

FULL SUN

8

(Picture 2) The open ground in this grassy meadow contains dandelions (gray seed heads) and buttercups (yellow flowers) in among the green grass.

▲ (Picture 3) The leaves and flowers of a water lily float on the still surface water of a pond.

to your home or school and looking at the common plants you find there. Then notice where they are common and where they are uncommon.

Look for the bright yellow dandelion, for example. You should find it on the school playing field, in your garden, or in a park.

What do all of these places have in common that a dandelion would like? They are open places with lots of sunshine. Dandelions cannot grow in the shade, so they choose a sunny place for their home (habitat) (Picture 2).

## Where water lilies live

Water lilies have large leaves that float on water. Many garden ponds have them. You can also see them in the ponds of parks (Picture 3).

If you look at a water lily, you will find it has long, floppy stalks. They are good for allowing the leaves to bob up and down in the water, but they do not have the strength to hold the plant up on dry land.

The water lily has roots, so the whole plant doesn't float. The water lily has its home (its habitat) in shallow ponds and swamps, not in deep open water.

### Summary
- A habitat is where something lives.
- You can find out about where plants live by studying the area where you find them.

Open areas have grass, buttercups, daisies, and dandelions.

Water lilies in pond.

WATER

# Finding out where animals live

**Even in a small area there will be many different kinds of places where animals live.**

It takes practice to spot where things live. Remember that a plant or an animal can live in an area of any size, and that this area will contain many other plants and animals. For example, a small piece of ground can provide a habitat for wood lice, beetles, and bees. They each live in a different part of the same area (Pictures 1 and 2), so they have different habitats.

## Where wood lice live

If you turn over a rotting piece of wood, you are likely to spot a wood louse (Picture 3). Wood lice like to live in wet, dark

▲ **(Picture 2) This beetle hunts along the ground and can be trapped using a sunken trap covered with moss. You should catch more beetles in places where they commonly live than in other places.**

▼ **(Picture 1) A small piece of ground provides a habitat for wood lice, beetles, and bees.**

Bumblebees visit flowers to get food for themselves and the nest.

Wood lice like shady, damp places to hide. They feed on rotting wood.

Ground beetles hunt among the shadows, hiding from birds that might eat them.

places (habitats). The wood is the source of food for the wood louse. Being wet makes the wood soft and easier to eat.

If you walked along a path, the chances are that you would never find a wood louse out in the open on dry ground.

You could test out this idea by keeping some wood lice in a tray with damp wood, some sand, and dry grass. Over a couple of days look to see where the wood lice are. This will give a clue as to the sort of place they like to live in. Then cover the tray over to make it dark. Lift off the cover, and see if the wood lice have ventured away from the wood. This will let you find out if they are more afraid of the light than the dry ground.

## Where bees live

Bees are common in summer, so it is easy to find out where they live. You will find bees moving among flowers in open ground, but you rarely find them in the shade under trees (Picture 4). That is because the bees are searching for food from flowers, and the flowers they are looking for are mainly found in the open. Open ground with flowers, like meadows, is the bees' habitat.

▶ (Picture 3) Wood lice have been found on the underside of this dead piece of wood.

▼ (Picture 4) Bees make their nest in a hole in the ground (bumblebees) or a hollow in a tree (honeybees), but they need a large area in which to find their food. So their habitat depends on finding both a suitable nest site and a large selection of flowers close by.

### Summary
- Each animal has its own kind of place where it lives.
- You can get some idea of where something lives by looking to see where you do and do not find it.

# Soil life

**A huge variety of life can be found in the upper layers of the soil.**

When you walk across open ground, you may think that there is nothing below your feet. But hidden out of sight in every soil there are huge numbers of animals that make the soil their home (Picture 1).

## Underground homes

Why would an animal want to live underground? Plants all have their roots in the soil. The surface of the ground is also where all dead leaves and seeds fall and where dead animals lie. This provides a plentiful supply of food for many creatures. The soil also gives shelter from the cold and heat.

But, of course, it is much more difficult to move around inside the soil than in the air or in water. So animals have to have special shapes that allow them to burrow.

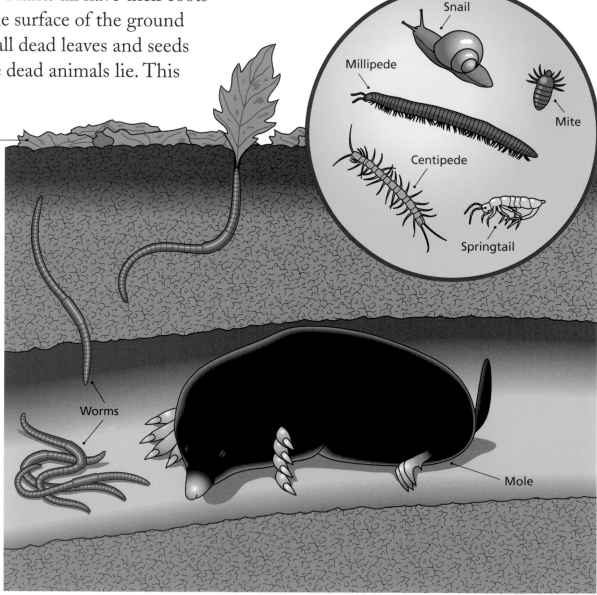

▶ (Picture 1) Animals that live in the soil and where you might find them.

Leaf litter

Worms

Mole

Snail

Millipede

Mite

Centipede

Springtail

If they are small, animals can also move around among the dead leaves and still keep largely out of sight.

## Where earthworms live

Earthworms eat dead plants and animals. They also burrow their way through the soil by eating it. An earthworm eats about its own weight of soil and food each day.

There is no point in an earthworm burrowing too deeply, however, because the deeper parts of soil contain less to eat. So the home (habitat) of an earthworm is in the soil just below the surface—the region we normally call the topsoil.

## Where springtails live

Springtails are tiny, wingless insects less than 10mm long. Many are able to spring from place to place, but mostly they crawl around in the leaves that rest on the soil. Springtails eat dead leaves, and so they live where the leaves are moist and soft. They do not eat the dried leaves on the surface.

## Where moles burrow

Moles are the most common large animals to live entirely in the soil. They eat earthworms and so make their home in the topsoil where the earthworms are to be found.

## Investigating the earthworm's home

You can dig out a section of moist soil using a trowel and put it in a glass jar.

Dead leaves

Sand

Garden soil

▲ (Picture 2) A jar is a suitable place to keep worms for a few days. Place a layer of soil at the bottom, then a layer of sand and a layer of leaves above it. Add two or three worms. You can see how the worms work as they mix the yellow sand with the brown soil.

Place a layer of sand in the jar, then a layer of moist, dead leaves. Place some earthworms on the surface. If you cover the sides of the jar with black paper and keep the soil moist, the earthworms will behave quite normally. If you remove the black paper from time to time, you can see just where the earthworms prefer to live (Picture 2).

### Summary
- Many animals live in the soil because it is sheltered.
- The soil surface is a rich source of food, and most animals live in the topsoil close to their food.

# Investigating variety

**The leaves of a tree or bush can be home to a wide variety of animals.**

A branch may seem to be a very exposed place to live, but in fact it is quite sheltered, and the leaves make a tasty meal for many small animals (Picture 1). You can see how full of life it is by gently shaking a branch over a tray (Picture 2). Many animals will fall out, but the

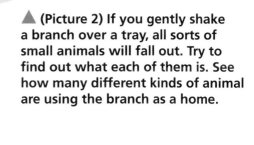

▲ (Picture 2) If you gently shake a branch over a tray, all sorts of small animals will fall out. Try to find out what each of them is. See how many different kinds of animal are using the branch as a home.

Earwig

Weevil

Ladybug

Caterpillar

Aphids

Leaf bug

Spider

▲ (Picture 1) Some of the small animals you might find on a branch in summer.

chances are you didn't notice any of them before they were shaken free. That is because many of the animals are a color similar to the leaves they use as a home.

## Plant-eaters

Some of the animals that live on branches eat leaves. Caterpillars are an example (Picture 3). Greenfly (aphids) suck the sap from the leaves. Earwigs are also common on branches. They eat leaves as well.

Many little beetles, such as weevils, can be found on branches too. Weevils are plant-eaters.

If you notice a small, black, ball-shaped thing stuck onto a leaf, then you have found a gall. It is where a small wasp lays an egg. It also causes the leaf to produce a swelling around the egg. That is the gall. The larva develops inside, protected by the hard gall.

## Hunters

The leaves are also home to animals that hunt. You may, for example, notice a ladybug. It is a hunter out to eat the aphids.

Lots of tiny spiders can be spotted as well. All spiders are hunters, trying to catch the plant-eaters while they graze.

▲ (Picture 3) If you find a caterpillar on a branch, you can keep it for a short while in a ventilated box with some of the leaves you found it on and some leaves from different trees. You can then look to see which leaves the caterpillar prefers to eat. In this way you can find out if it depends on a particular tree.

Of course, not everything that uses a branch as its home will fall when you shake it. Many birds live among the leaves. And now that you have seen how many animals there are in among the branches, you can see how birds can easily find enough to eat.

## Investigating the variety

If you gently shake branches from a number of bushes and trees growing in the same area over a tray, you will probably find different animals each time. This shows that many animals choose particular plants for their home.

### Summary
- Small plant-eating animals can make branches and leaves their home.
- Because plant-eating animals live on branches and leaves, they can be home for hunters, too.

# Living together

**Many plants and animals share the same living area. However, this can also mean danger.**

A nice, sunny rock close to a stream may be shared by many living things. For example, some small plants may grow on it, or it may be a resting place for dragonflies. But it is also a good place for lizards and other reptiles to sun themselves and warm up (Picture 1).

When you look around, you find many different kinds of living things. Each different kind of living thing is called a **SPECIES**. Species are groups that breed together. Each species that you see in an area is using that place as part of its home.

▼ (Picture 1) These terrapins are fish-eaters, so they live by lakes and rivers; but because they are cold-blooded, they also have to find sunny places to warm up.

## How many things can live together?

Every living thing has to choose a home where it can find food. In the case of plants this means that there has to be enough nourishment in the soil, sunlight, and water for their needs. Some plants need a lot of food and water, while others can live in areas with poor soils.

Animals have to find somewhere with enough plants or other animals to eat. Some animals will eat many different types of plants or animals; others eat only one type of food. The panda, for example, eats just bamboo, while most bears will eat fruit, insects, fish, and other animals.

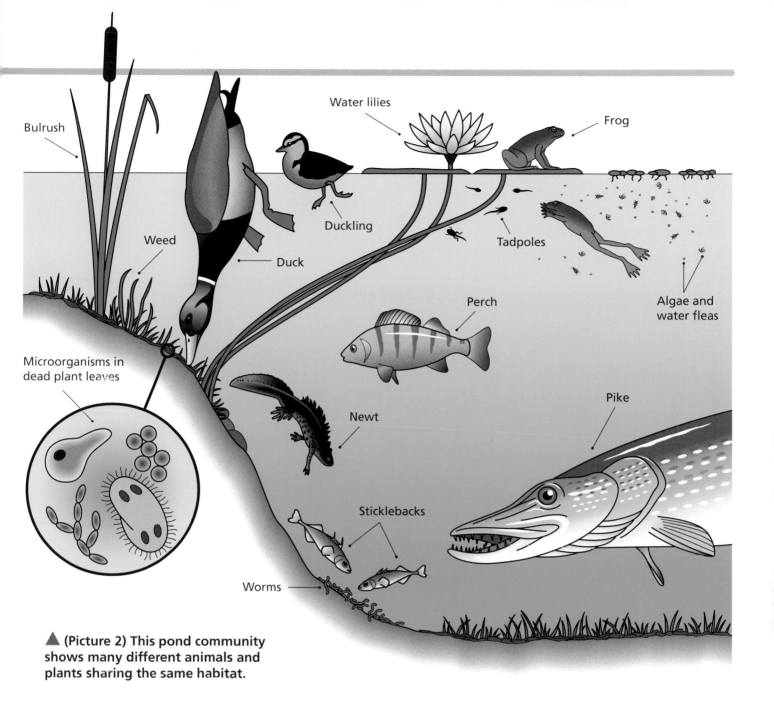

Bulrush

Water lilies

Frog

Weed

Duckling

Duck

Tadpoles

Algae and
water fleas

Perch

Microorganisms in
dead plant leaves

Newt

Pike

Sticklebacks

Worms

▲ (Picture 2) This pond community
shows many different animals and
plants sharing the same habitat.

In general, a place where there is a good soil, warm, sunny conditions, and enough water will be home to many living things. This means that many plants or animals of the same kind will live there.

## Communities

All of the living things in an area make up a **COMMUNITY**. The community is entirely self-contained. It does not need anything from outside except water, air, and sunlight. So communities of plants and animals can all share the same home (habitat) (Picture 2).

### Summary

- Many plants and animals can share the same home.
- A group of plants and animals living together is called a community.

# Food chains

**Many of the plants and animals that live together in a community depend on each other as a source of food or to help them breed.**

All life must eat to survive. As a result, each of the species in a community must find enough to eat. They must also breed to continue the species.

## Plants

Plants produce their food from the soil, water, and air. They produce more living material than anything else in the community. Plants need animals to help carry their pollen between plants and to carry their seeds to new areas where they can grow.

## Plant-eating animals

No other living things can make their food from the materials around them. Instead, they must eat either plants or other animals. Many animals eat plants, either the leaves, roots, or seeds.

## Hunters

Some animals are not able to get the nourishment they need from plants. Instead, they must eat other animals. They are called hunters. The food for the hunters may be other meat-eating animals, or it may be plant-eating animals.

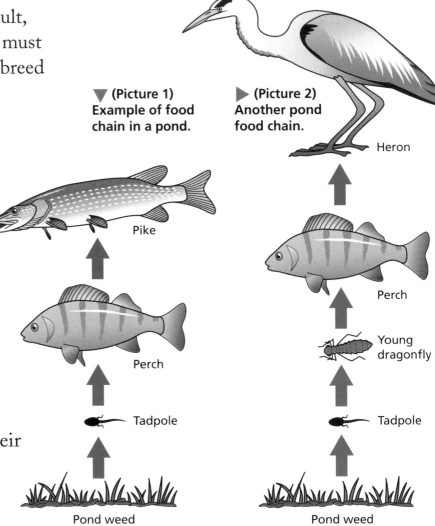

▼ **(Picture 1)** Example of food chain in a pond.

▶ **(Picture 2)** Another pond food chain.

Heron

Pike

Perch

Perch

Young dragonfly

Tadpole

Tadpole

Pond weed

Pond weed

## Food chain

As you can see, in nature there is a long line of animals, each depending on another animal or a plant for its food. Scientists call this a **FOOD CHAIN**.

Picture 1 shows a typical food chain for part of a pond:

**Pond weed ➤ tadpole ➤ perch ➤ pike**

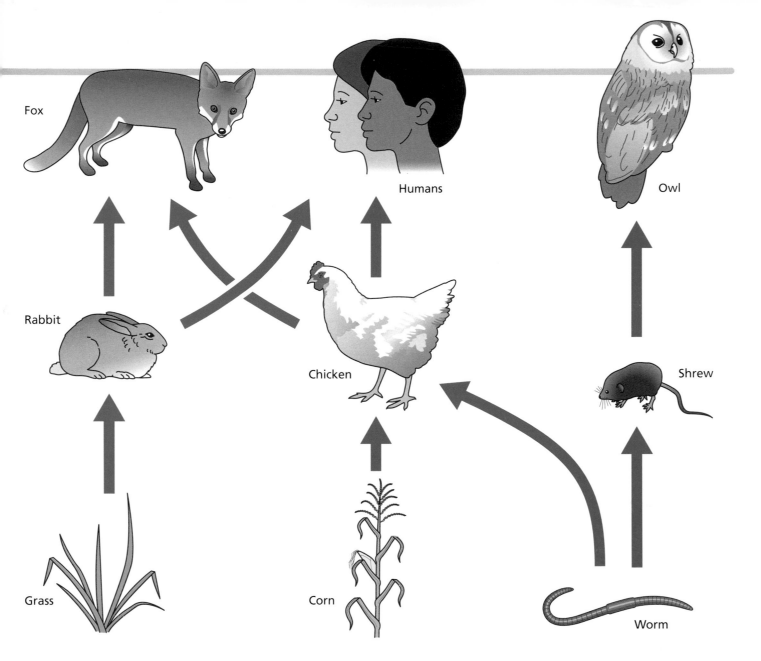

Fox

Humans

Owl

Rabbit

Chicken

Shrew

Grass

Corn

Worm

Notice that the plant is on the left when the chain is written in words, and the pike (the last link in the chain) is on the right.

Any community will have lots of food chains. Picture 2 shows another pond example:

**Pond weed ➤ tadpole ➤ young dragonfly ➤ perch ➤ heron**

▲ (Picture 3) Examples of food chains on land. Some animals belong to more than one food chain. This is shown by the cross-over arrows.

There are also many food chains on land. Picture 3 shows three examples, one of which includes us.

## Summary
• Animals and plants depend on one another.
• A group of plants and animals that depend on one another is linked into a food chain.

## Harder words
You may want to remember these words:
• Plant-eating animals are called HERBIVORES.
• Meat-eating animals are called CARNIVORES.
• Animals that hunt other animals are called PREDATORS.
• Animals that are hunted are called PREY.

# Changes in food chains

**When rivers are cleaned out, the habitats for many living things may be lost.**

Rivers are a common part of our landscape. But they can be changed dramatically. This happens when people get worried about rivers flooding, want to use rivers for boats, or want to use the fertile land near the river for farming.

## Natural rivers and riverbanks

Picture 1 shows a part of a meandering river that has been undisturbed by humans. You can find a large variety of animals here, and you should be able to make out some food chains. The main

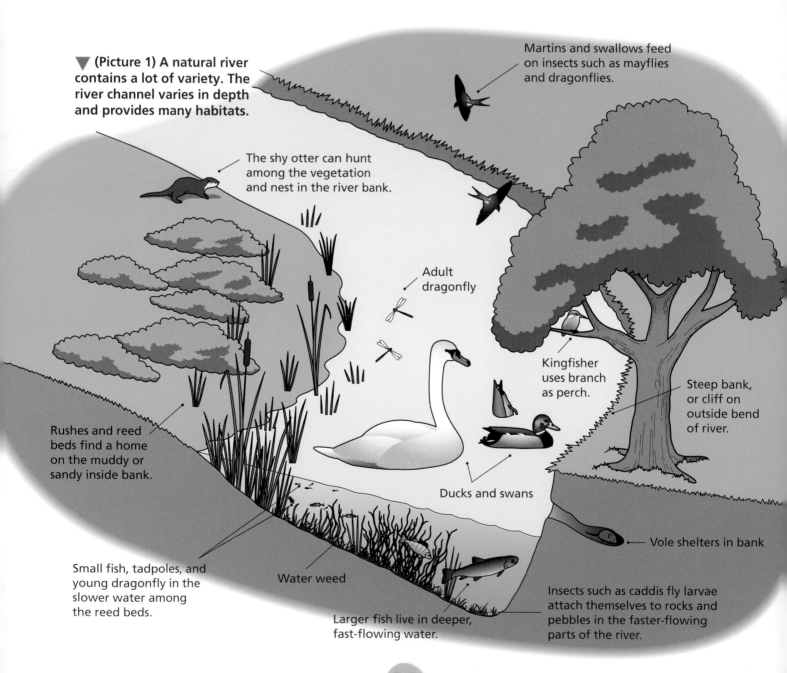

▼ **(Picture 1) A natural river contains a lot of variety. The river channel varies in depth and provides many habitats.**

Martins and swallows feed on insects such as mayflies and dragonflies.

The shy otter can hunt among the vegetation and nest in the river bank.

Adult dragonfly

Kingfisher uses branch as perch.

Steep bank, or cliff on outside bend of river.

Rushes and reed beds find a home on the muddy or sandy inside bank.

Ducks and swans

Vole shelters in bank

Small fish, tadpoles, and young dragonfly in the slower water among the reed beds.

Water weed

Larger fish live in deeper, fast-flowing water.

Insects such as caddis fly larvae attach themselves to rocks and pebbles in the faster-flowing parts of the river.

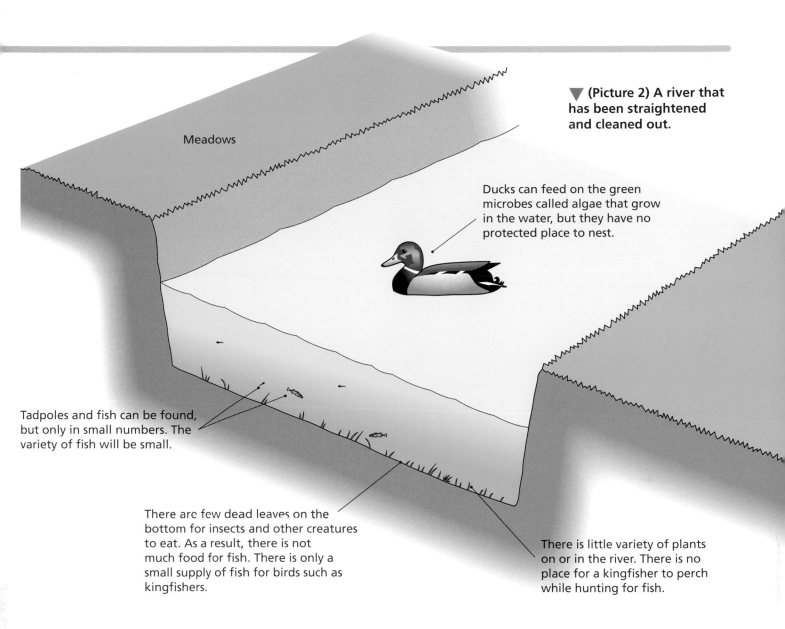

▼ (Picture 2) A river that has been straightened and cleaned out.

Meadows

Ducks can feed on the green microbes called algae that grow in the water, but they have no protected place to nest.

Tadpoles and fish can be found, but only in small numbers. The variety of fish will be small.

There are few dead leaves on the bottom for insects and other creatures to eat. As a result, there is not much food for fish. There is only a small supply of fish for birds such as kingfishers.

There is little variety of plants on or in the river. There is no place for a kingfisher to perch while hunting for fish.

features are the fast- and slow-flowing areas, deep and shallow areas, and open and shaded areas. It is this variety that gives many different species a chance to thrive.

## Changing channels

Engineers sometimes straighten and dredge rivers because they believe it will make flooding less likely. They scrape the banks clear and smooth out the bed. This makes a channel that carries water away more quickly (it makes a large open drain). But the shelter and variety of places for

wildlife are reduced, and this means that fewer plants and animals can live in such a place. You will find that many of the food chains in Picture 1 have links missing in Picture 2. Once one link is missing, the whole chain may collapse, and other creatures die.

### Summary
- A natural landscape has a wide variety of habitats for plants and animals.
- A managed landscape can lose most of its habitats, making it difficult for many species to survive.

# Improving the environment for living things

By making country parks, we can turn empty space into places where many species can thrive.

In towns and countryside there are many areas of wasteland. They may be old factory sites, coal mines, or gravel pits, for example. Once they are abandoned, a few species survive; but by making careful changes, these areas can teem with wildlife. All that is needed is to understand what homes (habitats) wildlife needs.

## Designing a country park

Most of us have a country park nearby. Nearly all of them are on reclaimed land (Picture 1). Suppose you had to think about turning an area of wasteland into

▶ **(Picture 1) The plan for a simple country park based on an abandoned area of coal-mining or disused gravel pits.**

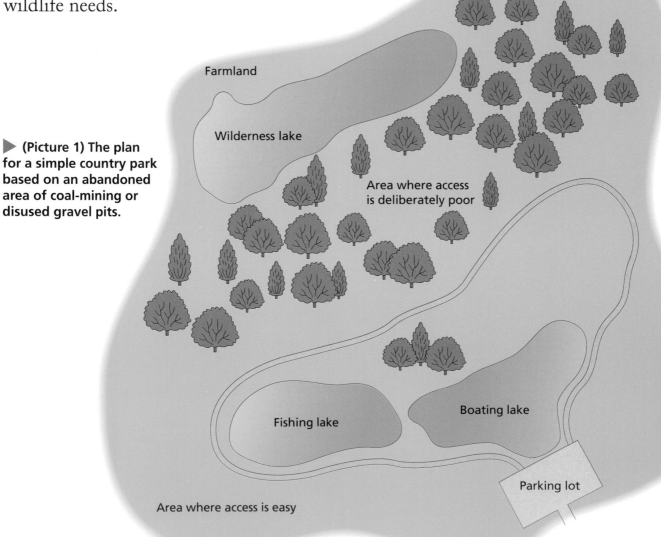

Farmland

Wilderness lake

Area where access is deliberately poor

Fishing lake

Boating lake

Parking lot

Area where access is easy

a place that both people and wildlife can enjoy. What would you do?

From the previous pages in this book you can see that some living things need open ground, some need woodland, and others need ponds or rivers. Some need dry soil, while others need moist soil. There has to be enough variety to attract different animals and make food chains. Most wildlife also needs to have some protection from people.

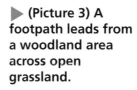 (Picture 2) An artificial island has been left in this old gravel pit to make a safe home for some waterbirds.

▶ (Picture 3) A footpath leads from a woodland area across open grassland.

## Plan for variety

You can make all of these possible, even in a small area. The key idea is to make the place as varied as possible (Picture 2). If a part was dug out to make a pond or a lake, any spare soil could make some small hills. With this simple step you have created lots of different types of land for different species to thrive.

If the hills are now planted with trees, then you have the start of a woodland. Leaving strips of land without trees creates open ground for those species that need it.

Adding a path that goes into part of the woodland, across some open ground (Picture 3), and beside part of the pond or lake completes the simple plan. This makes it easier for people to visit and also makes it more likely that they will not go on the rest of the land. In this way much of the land is left almost undisturbed for the shy creatures to live in.

With these simple steps both people and wildlife can thrive.

### Summary
- Wasteland can be used for people and wildlife.
- By making the land varied, you can make lots of habitats, even in a small area.

# Index

## Science Matters!

### Grolier Educational

First published in the United States in 2003 by Grolier Educational, Sherman Turnpike, Danbury, CT 06816

Copyright © 2003
Atlantic Europe Publishing Company Ltd.

*All rights reserved. No part of this publication may be reproduced, stored in a retrieval system, or transmitted in any form or by any means—electronic, mechanical, photocopying, recording, or otherwise—without prior permission of the publisher.*

*This product is manufactured from sustainable managed forests. For every tree cut down at least one more is planted.*

**Author**
*Brian Knapp, BSc, PhD*

**Educational Consultant**
*Peter Riley, BSc, C Biol, MI Biol, PGCE*

**Art Director**
*Duncan McCrae, BSc*

**Senior Designer**
*Adele Humphries, BA, PGCE*

**Editor**
*Lisa Magloff, BA*

**Illustrations**
*David Woodroffe*

**Designed and produced by**
*Earthscape Editions*

**Reproduced in Malaysia by**
*Global Color*

**Printed in Hong Kong by**
*Wing King Tong Company Ltd*

**Picture credits**
All photographs are from the Earthscape Editions photolibrary.

**Library of Congress Cataloging-in-Publication Data**
Knapp, Dr. Brian J.
    Science Matters! / [Dr. Brian J. Knapp].
        p. cm.
    Includes index.
    Summary: Presents information on a wide variety of topics in basic biology, chemistry, and physics.
    Contents: v. 1. Food, teeth, and eating—v. 2. Helping plants grow well—v. 3. Properties of materials—v. 4. Rocks and soils—v. 5. Springs and magnets—v. 6. Light and shadows—v. 7. Moving and growing—v. 8. Habitats—v. 9. Keeping warm and cool—v. 10. Solids and liquids—v. 11. Friction—v. 12. Simple electricity—v. 13. Keeping healthy—v. 14. Life cycles—v. 15. Gases around us—v. 16. Changing from solids to liquids to gases—v. 17. Earth and beyond—v. 18. Changing sounds—v. 19. Adapting and surviving—v. 20. Microbes—v. 21. Dissolving—v. 22. Changing materials—v. 23. Forces in action—v. 24. How we see things—v. 25. Changing circuits.
    ISBN 0-7172-5834-3 (set)—ISBN 0-7172-5835-1 (v. 1)—ISBN 0-7172-5836-X (v. 2)—ISBN 0-7172-5837-8 (v. 3)—ISBN 0-7172-5838-6 (v. 4)—ISBN 0-7172-5839-4 (v. 5)—ISBN 0-7172-5840-8 (v. 6)—ISBN 0-7172-5841-6 (v. 7)—ISBN 0-7172-5842-4 (v. 8)—ISBN 0-7172-5843-2 (v. 9)—ISBN 0-7172-5844-0 (v. 10)—ISBN 0-7172-5845-9 (v. 11)—ISBN 0-7172-5846-7 (v. 12)—ISBN 0-7172-5847-5 (v. 13)—ISBN 0-7172-5848-3 (v. 14)—ISBN 0-7172-5849-1 (v. 15)—ISBN 0-7172-5850-5 (v. 16)—ISBN 0-7172-5851-3 (v. 17)—ISBN 0-7172-5852-1 (v. 18)—ISBN 0-7172-5853-X (v. 19)—ISBN 0-7172-5854-8 (v. 20)—ISBN 0-7172-5855-6 (v. 21)—ISBN 0-7172-5856-4 (v. 22)—ISBN 0-7172-5857-2 (v. 23)—ISBN 0-7172-5858-0 (v. 24)—ISBN 0-7172-5859-9 (v. 25)
    1. Science—Juvenile literature. [1. Science.] I. Title.

Q163.K48 2002
500—dc21

2002017302